The Shipwreck

Written by
Rob Waring and **Maurice Jamall**

Before You Read

to breathe

to die

to dive

to hear

to pull

to swim

air

anchor

dolphin

island

octopus

shark

treasure chest

water (sea)

In the story

David

John

Faye

Tyler

Daniela

John, Daniela, Faye, David and Tyler have a boat. They are all friends. Sometimes they go swimming, and sometimes they go fishing. Today, they are going to Shark Island by boat. They want to go diving and swimming.

Faye is looking at a notice. She says, "Are there any sharks at Shark Island?"

She is talking to her friend, John. He is sitting next to her. "No, I don't think so," he says.

"Good," replies Faye. "I don't like sharks."

It is a very good day to go out in their boat. They take their boat out to sea. They stop near Shark Island. Faye puts the anchor in the water.

Daniela says, "This is a great place. This is going to be fun."

"Let's swim," says John. "Who's coming in the water? The water will be great!"

"I'm ready. I'm coming," answers David.

"Well, umm . . . Not today, thanks. I'm not going in.
I'll wait here," says Faye. "Maybe another day.
The water looks too cold."
"I'll swim with you later," says Daniela.
David says to John, "Great! Let's look for some fish."
"Okay," replies John. "Let's look over there," he says.
John and David dive down into the water. They are
strong swimmers.

David and John swim for a long time. They dive under the water. They see some beautiful fish. They look for some shells. "Wow! Look at these shells," thinks John. "It's so great here," thinks David. He is very excited. They are having a great time.

Faye looks in the water. She sees something. It's big and grey. "That's strange," she says.

"What's strange?" asks Daniela.

"There's something big in the water," she replies.

Daniela smiles and says, "Maybe it's David."

"Don't say that!" says Faye, but she laughs.

Then Faye sees something big in the water. "Look!
What's that?" shouts Faye. Tyler sees it, too.
"Look out! John! John! There's a shark!" shouts Tyler.
"A shark!" John does not hear because he is swimming.
He cannot see the shark.
"John! Come back, come back!" shouts Faye. She is very
worried about John.
"John! John!" she shouts again.

John hears Faye. He looks behind him and sees the shark! He starts swimming back to the boat very quickly. David is looking at the shark. He does not say anything. Then he looks at the shark. "That's strange," says David. He has an idea. "David, what's strange? What are you doing?" asks Faye.
"Don't worry. It's okay," he says.

Suddenly, David dives into the water. Faye is very shocked!
"No! David! There's a shark. Don't go!" shouts Faye.
"Stop!! It's dangerous!"
David does not listen. He swims out to sea. He swims to the shark. Everybody is really worried about David.
"What's he doing?" asks Tyler.

David swims to the shark. The shark swims to David.
"David! It's a shark! A shark! Come back!" shouts Tyler.
"You're swimming the wrong way!"
"Come back!!" calls Daniela.
David does not listen. He swims and swims. John gets
to the boat. Faye helps him get into the boat.
"Are you okay?" asks Faye.
"Quick, get me in the boat," says John.

It is not a shark! It is a dolphin!

"Look at the dolphin," says David. "Isn't it great?" He swims with the dolphin to the boat.

"Oh, David! It's a dolphin!" says Faye. "You didn't tell us, David. Why? We were so worried."

"It's okay, Faye. Of course, I knew it was a dolphin! Sharks look different," says David.

Faye is angry with David. "But David, why didn't you tell us?" she asks.

David laughs and says, "Faye, you were really funny. You were so scared!"

"Faye, it wasn't a shark. It was a dolphin. You really scared me," says John angrily. "That was really bad of you. Never do that again, Faye," he says.

Faye says, "I'm sorry, John, but I was so worried. I didn't know it was a dolphin."

"It's okay," he says. "Be careful next time, please."

"Okay, I'm sorry," says Faye again.

"Come in the water, John. Faye, Daniela come in," says David happily. "Come and swim with the dolphins."

"Yeah, okay. I'll swim with them," says John.
Faye says, "Be careful!"
"Don't worry so much Faye! I'll be okay," says John.
He dives into the water. David and John swim with
the dolphins. Two more dolphins come to them.
"It's a family of dolphins!" John says.

14

John and David swim with the dolphins. They are having a great time. The dolphins pull the boys through the water. They jump high into the air. They dive under the water. Everybody watches them play. Tyler gives a small fish to a dolphin.

"Look at them, they are really great," says Daniela.

"Yes, they are," replies Faye.

John and David dive down under the water. John sees something. "What's that?" he thinks. He shows David and he understands.

"It's an old ship!" thinks David. They both swim to the old ship.

"It's an old shipwreck," thinks John. "Wow, I love this place," he thinks. The dolphins swim with them.

The dolphins take David and John down to see the ship.
The dolphins can swim very fast.
"This is great," thinks David. "I want to tell the others about this."
"Wow! This is so good!" thinks John.
They look at the old ship. There are some very old things. There are an old anchor, some old ropes, a lamp and many more things.

John swims to the back of the ship. He wants to look in it. He finds the name of the boat. It is *Lady Grey*.

"Wow, this ship is very old!" he thinks. "It's really great!" The dolphin takes David back to get some more air.

John finds an old chest near the ship. It is a big old treasure chest. He shows it to David.
"Wow! What's in there?" he thinks. "There may be some treasure in it. Today is our lucky day!"
David and John want to look in the treasure chest. The dolphins take them down to it.

David and John push open the chest. There is a big octopus in the chest! David does not see the octopus. It takes his leg. "Oh no!" thinks David. "It has my leg. How am I going to get back to the boat?"
John and David hit the octopus, but it still has David's leg. It does not let him go.

John hits the octopus hard. But the octopus still has David's leg. He cannot move. David is in big trouble. John cannot help David because he has only a little air. The dolphins take John up to the boat. David cannot breathe. Nobody can help him.

"I'm going to die," he thinks. "I must get to the boat! I don't have much time."

David is in danger. He tries to get away from the octopus, but he cannot. Faye follows John down to help David. Suddenly, a dolphin hits the octopus. It is very surprised. It lets go of David's leg. Faye, John and the dolphins take David back to the boat.

Faye and John help David to get in the boat. They are all worried. David is okay now.

"David!" says Daniela. "David! Are you okay?"

Everybody is very worried about him. He is very tired. He cannot say anything.

"Will he be okay?" asks John.

"Yes, I think so," says Faye. "We must get him home."

Later, David feels better. David and John thank the dolphins for their help.

"David, you were very lucky. Do you feel okay now?" asks Daniela.

David replies, "No, not really. But I'll be okay soon, I think."

"That was great!" says John.

"Not for me!" says David. "But I want to come back!"